Hindu
Gods & Goddesses

Hindu
Gods
&
Goddesses

Sunita Pant Bansal

SMRITI BOOKS
NEW DELHI, INDIA

ISBN:81-87967-72-2

First Edition: 2005

© Text: Smriti Books®
Photographs courtesy:
Avdhesh Bansal
Paintings courtesy:
Archaeological Survey of India, New
Delhi, India
Ashutosh Museum, Kolkata University,
West Bengal, India
Bharat Kala Bhavan, Uttar Pradesh, India
British Museum, London, UK
Collection Villiers David, London, UK
India Office Library, London, UK
National Archives, New Delhi, India
National Museum, New Delhi, India
University of Kashmir Valley,
Kashmir, India
Victoria and Albert Museum London,
UK

Designer: Sujith VM

Published by: ®
SMRITI BOOKS®
124 Siddharth Enclave
New Delhi 110014
India
Email: mail@smritibooks.com

Printed by:
Gopsons Papers Ltd, New Delhi, India

About the book

Hindu Gods & Goddesses is an endeavour to make available the basic information about the Hindu pantheon of gods in a simple and attractive manner. The basics are told without getting into the religiosity of the same. No recommendations are made for any one deity, keeping in mind the fundamental Hindu philosophy of the oneness of the entire universe.

Information about the origin of each deity, its various forms, relationship with other deities, and the important shrines, is given in a condensed manner. There is a deliberate variety in the visuals of the book, to highlight the diversity in the understanding of the individuals. It has also added a lot of colour and ethnic charm to the crisp text. Effort has been made to source as many Indian art forms as possible: sculptures of stone, wood, metal, clay, miniatures, pattachitra, madhubani, tanjore, phad, kalamkari, warli, etc to show the unifying principle underlying the work of the various artists. Unity in diversity has always been the strength of Hindustan.

Contents

Introduction

Hinduism is often labeled as a religion of 330 million gods. This misunderstanding arises when people fail to grasp the symbolism of the Hindu pantheon. Just as a single force in space can be mathematically conceived as having various spatial components, the Supreme Being or God, the personal form of the Ultimate Reality, is conceived by Hindus as having various aspects. It is the same with all the gods and goddesses: they are not rivals but aspects of a single principle. Hindus have represented God in innumerable forms. Each is but a symbol that points to a particular aspect; and as none exhausts God's actual nature, the entire array is needed to complete the picture of God's aspects and manifestations. It has been said that images are to the Hindu worshipper what diagrams are to the geometrician. The Hindu devotee, while he will generally have one particular form of god - his or her *ishta deva*, or chosen deity - on whom his devotion centres, moves easily between one god and another. Collectively the pantheon of gods portrays the Hindu concept of the Supreme Being expressed as 'Om'. This mystic syllable encompasses all that is sacred in Hinduism, the universal soul, the Brahman.

But the creator of life, the Brahma was *Nirguna*, without form, abstract and intangible. People wanting to express themselves to the creator felt lost, as they needed a semblance of 'The Brahman' to whom they could offer their prayers. So the *Nirguna Brahman* evolved into *Saguna Brahman*. 'The Brahman' appeared as a male trinity, a three faced God called 'Trimurti'.

The Trimurti has a human form, one body with three heads that express the cycle of life, with Brahma the creator of the Universe, Vishnu the preserver, maintaining *dharma* (righteousness) and order and Shiva the destroyer. Even the Trimurti evolved as each of the gods found celestial consorts

(goddesses in their own right). Brahma's consort is Saraswati, the goddess of learning. Lakshmi, the goddess of wealth, Vishnu's and Parvati is Shiva's consort. And the family continued to grow

Thus God grew from a primordial 'Om' into an infinite pantheon of gods, worshipped devoutly by infinite believers.

Vedic Gods

People of the Indus Valley Civilisation (3,000 to 1,500 BC), prayed to Mother Goddess. Ritual and religion played a large part in their daily life. The famous Mohenjodaro statue of the Priest King affirms the primal power conferred on a religious leader. Seals engraved with inscriptions of animals avow the ancient veneration of the cow. Fire and trees were also worshipped.

The Aryans from Central Asia invaded India (about 1,500 BC). Their religion consisted of the worship of the powers of nature. The Vedas, a collection of hymns were composed in pre-classical Sanskrit during the second millennium BC.

These Vedic hymns created the first stage of Hindu mythology. The original Veda is the Rig Veda. The Yajur-Veda, Sama-Veda, and Atharva-Veda, were composed later. The hymns addressed the elements: Surya (the Sun), Agni (fire), Indra (thunder), Vayu (the Wind) and Varuna (Ocean).

The elements were the early gods, of whom Surya, the sun-god, is the most important. Golden coloured Surya rides a chariot drawn by seven red mares, each named for a day of the week. His twin sons, the Ashvins often precede him in their golden chariot. The *swastika* is the sign of Surya, a symbol of his generosity. The direction of the *swastika* indicates the four cardinal directions in which sticks are placed for Vedic sacrificial fires.

Agni, the fire-god was worshipped with great devotion. His seven arms span the seven continents. He is portrayed with an extended stomach representing his ability to devour. He is coloured red and rides a ram. His tongue is a flame that licks up sacrificial *ghee*. Sacrifice was a central concept to the Aryan religion and fire played an important role. Present in every dwelling of the rich or the poor, Agni was the *sakshi* (witness) of all the holy rituals, sacrifices, marriage and the funereal rites. During a Vedic wedding

11

ceremony the bride and groom walk around the fire seven times to sanctify their marriage, for Agni is considered witness and representative of all gods.

Indra, the god of the sky, rainmaker, bearer of thunder and conductor of lightning, was the creator of storms with his Vajra (thunderbolt). Indra has a white elephant called Airavat. He rides in a golden chariot drawn by horses whose flying manes imply the speed with which they draw him. Indra's weapons are the Vajra, bow (the rainbow), net and a hook. As weather-god and sustainer of life he battles against the god of drought and death. Hindus aspire to live in Swarga (heaven) with Indra after death, for despite his dazzling weapons Indra is a peaceful god, who offers refuge to all who follow the path of *dharma* (righteousness).

Vayu is the god of the wind. He is the father of the monkey-god Hanuman and of the Pandava prince Bhima. Flighty and swift he often carried Indra through the skies. His mount is a deer and he carries a wheel in his hand as a symbol for speed. Vayu is revered for he signifies a vital sign of life - breath. Vayu is also called Pavan, one who enlivens *prakriti* (nature). As Pavan, he is the bearer of life dispersing seeds. He scatters pollen to bring flowers to bloom and permeates the air with floral perfumes.

Varuna is the god of the oceans. He is the element *vari* (water). His chariot is drawn by the fluid strength of ocean waves. Varuna was the earlier rainmaker, until Indra took over his function. Under the oceans Varuna lives in an underwater palace called Pushpagiri (mountain of flowers). His mount is a fish

called Makara. In the oldest hymns he was described as the creator. He fixed the orbits for planets and the directions of the winds and the flight of the birds.

The Vedic gods were worshipped with prayer and sacrifice. Their very conception was Aryan, most of the gods drove chariots drawn by horses. The Aryans had introduced the horse to India. The highest sacrifice was the Ashvamedha (the Horse Sacrifice). When a king had no male heir, he would consign his finest stallion to the flames. His wives would then spend the night close to the smouldering remains of the carcass. It was believed that the spirit of the animal would make the queens fertile. The Aryans also believed that a hundred such Ashvamedhas would make the king, the emperor of the world.

Divine Mother

The worship of God in the form of Mother is a unique feature of Hinduism. Today Hindus worship the Divine Mother in many popular forms such as Durga, Kali, Lakshmi, Saraswati, Ambika and Uma.

In the most representative Hindu view, the universe is the manifestation of the creative power (*shakti*) of Brahman. In Hinduism, Divine Mother is the first manifestation of Divine Energy. Thus with the name of Divine Mother comes the idea of energy, omnipotence, omnipresence, love, intelligence and wisdom. Just as a child believes its mother to be all-powerful, and capable of doing anything for the child, a devotee believes the Divine Mother to be all merciful, all-powerful and eternally guiding and protecting him with her invisible arms.

Planet Deities

The nine planet deities are also referred to as Nava (nine) Grahas (planets). These *grahas* are supposed to have a significant impact on the lives of an individual. Classical Vedic astrology uses seven visible planets; the Sun, Moon, Mars, Mercury, Jupiter, Venus and Saturn, along with the two lunar nodes, the north and south nodes, Rahu and Ketu.

Sun or Surya is a living god, whom everyone can see and pray to. He is the life-giver and according to the Vedas he is a witness (*sakshi*) to all actions. Angaraka or Mars is regarded as a god of martial character, red in every aspect. Brihaspati or Jupiter is revered as the Guru of *devas*, and protector of the world.

Buddha or Mercury is considered as the greatest among the wise. This god bestows wisdom and wealth. Chief among *gyanis* (realized souls) he is considered Vishnu *roopi*, because of his beauty. Chandra or Moon is a lovable and loving god. Sages and devotees invoke the Goddess Mother (radiating *amrit* to strengthen the mind) in Chandra and meditate for hours. Lunar and solar eclipses are said to occur because of Rahu and Ketu. Shani or Saturn is a protector that may turn destroyer if angry.

Shukra or Venus is the bestower of long life, wealth, happiness, children, property and good education. He is the Guru of *asuras*. A beneficial god, he blesses the devotees with power to control one's *indriyas* (sense organs) and enables the devotees to obtain fame and name.

Animal Deities

Hindus see divinity in all living creatures. Animal deities therefore, occupy an important place in Hindu *dharma*. Animals have been used by the gods as forms of transport, and hence revered by man. Each deity has a particular vehicle on which he or she travels. These vehicles, which are either animals or birds, represent the various forces that he or she rides. Goddess Saraswati's vehicle, the graceful and beautiful peacock denotes that she is the controller of the pursuit of performing arts. Vishnu sits on the primal serpent, which represents the desire of consciousness in humankind. Shiva rides the Nandi bull, which stands for the brute and blind power, as well as the unbridled sexual energy in man - the qualities only he can help us control. His consort Parvati, Durga or Kali rides on a lion, which symbolizes mercilessness, anger and pride - vices she can help her devotees keep in check. Ganesha's carrier, a mouse represents the timidity and nervousness that overwhelm us at the onset of any new venture - feelings that can be overcome by the blessings of Ganesha.

Other than the vehicles, certain animals are revered in their own right as having a celestial connection. Airavat, the king-god of elephants, is the mount of Lord Indra. This elephant emerged out of the waters when the ocean was churned by the gods. That is why the name is derived from *Iravat*, (one produced by water). He is also called Ardh-Matana (elephant of the clouds), Arkasodara (brother of the sun), Naga-Malla (the fighting elephant). Airavat has four tusks, and is white in colour.

Garuda, a bird deity, with the head and wings of an eagle and sometimes with the rest of his body like that of a man, is called the king of birds and he is also the carrier of Lord Vishnu. Garuda is also known by another name Vinayaka, which he shares with Lord Ganesha. Thus, this god-bird is thought to be remover of obstacles. Garuda is not separately worshipped as an independent god. He is worshipped together with Vishnu. His image is placed near Vishnu in temples and in pictures he is depicted carrying Vishnu in the skies on its back. The elder brother of Garuda is Urud or Aruna, who is the charioteer of Surya, the Sun God. Garuda's son is Jatayu, who tried to rescue Sita, when Ravana was fleeing after kidnapping her.

Kamdhenu, the sacred cow deity is considered to grant all wishes and desires. It is believed that she emerged from *Samudra-manthan* (the churning of the ocean) and taken away by seven gods, who comprise the constellation of the Great Bear in the sky. Mother of all cows, she is also called Surabhi, Shaval, Aditi and Kamduh. Shesh Naag, the serpent god, has been venerated and worshipped by many for centuries. He is considered to be the king of infernal regions called Patal. Lord Vishnu sleeps over the bed of its coils during intervals of creation. Shesh Naag is also represented as one supporting the world on its hood.

Agni	» ram
Brahma	» swan
Durga	» lion
Ganesha	» mouse
Indra	» elephant
Kartikeya	» peacock
Lakshmi	» owl
Maheshwari	» bull
Saraswati	» swan or peacock
Shiva	» Nandi, the bull
Surya	» seven horses
Varuna	» seven swans
Vayu	» thousand horses
Vishnu	» Garuda, the eagle and Shesh Naag, the serpent
Vishwakarma	» elephant
Yama	» male buffalo

Brahma
Lord of Creation

Brahma, the creator of the universe, was born from *Hiranyagarbha* (the golden nucleus). When he took form, Brahma placed the *Hiranyagarbha* back in the waters and inspired the creation of the universe. Every living being in the universe originates from him and is an aspect of Brahma.

Brahma's consort is Saraswati (goddess of ultimate knowledge). When Saraswati and Brahma embrace they create the world. Together, they thus introduce the soul into the cycle of life. Saraswati is the goddess of wisdom and science, the mother of the Vedas, and the inventor of the Devanagari script. She is represented as a fair woman with four arms, dressed in white and seated on a white lotus. As goddess of the arts, she is shown playing or holding a *veena*. In one of her right hands, she holds a book of palm leaves, and in the other, a lotus. In her left hands, she has a string of pearls, and a *damaru*.

A day in the life of Brahma is a *kalpa*, which encompasses a span of evolution. Each *kalpa* measures four billion human years. As Prajapati (creator), while he is awake the world forms, while he sleeps all shrinks to a dormant nucleus. Late Vedic literature describes Brahma as creator of Soma and Surya (Sun and Moon), he gives them their place in the sky. He brings Agni (fire) into being and sets Vayu (wind) free to roam the world and makes Varuna (water) spring to life on earth.

There are no temples for Brahma (except one in Pushkar, Rajasthan) as for Shiva and Vishnu, for there has been no separate cult for Brahma as the Shaiva or Vaishnava cults.

According to mythology, Brahma is supposed to have been cursed by Shiva (for having uttered a lie and for his ego) that he would go without worship. Yet in all Shiva and Vishnu temples, there is an image of Lord Brahma on the northern wall and he is one of the important *parivara devata* (attendant deity).

Originally, Brahma is said to have five heads. The Matsya Purana explains the reason for this. It states that Brahma created a woman, known by different names: Satarupa, Saraswati, Sandhya or Brahmi.

Because of her beauty, he fell in love with her and stared at her longingly.

To avoid his gaze, she moved to his left, then behind him, and then to his right. But a head sprang up wherever she moved to enable Brahma to continue looking at her. In desperation, she jumped into the air, but a fifth head appeared on top. Brahma then asked her to help him create the universe. He lived with her for a hundred divine years at the end of which Manu was born.

There are different explanations for why Brahma only has four heads now, as opposed to his original five. According to the Puranas, Brahma and Vishnu were once arguing over who was superior of the two. Once they realized that

Shiva was the Supreme Being, Brahma however, spoke disparagingly about Shiva. In anger, Shiva cut off the head, which had spoken, and therefore Brahma was left with four heads.

Brahma is usually represented as a bearded, four-faced, four-armed, red-coloured deity. He carries a rosary in the upper right hand, a book in the upper left hand, a *kamandal* (water pot) in the lower left hand, and bestows grace with his lower right hand. The four faces represent the sacred knowledge of the four Vedas (Rig, Yajur, Sama, and Atharva) symbolizing that Brahma is the source of all knowledge necessary for the creation of the universe. The four arms represent the four directions and thus represent the omnipresence and omnipotence of Lord Brahma. Unlike other deities, Brahma does not have a weapon.

The rosary symbolizes the time cycle through which the world moves from creation to sustenance, from sustenance to dissolution, and from dissolution to new creation. The rosary also symbolizes the materials used in the process of creation. Its position in the back right hand suggests the intelligent use of these materials in the process of creation.

A book in the back hand (symbolizing the intellect) illustrates that right knowledge is important for any kind of creative work. A water pot (*kamandal*) in the front left hand symbolizes the cosmic energy by which Brahma brings the universe into existence. The hand symbolizing ego (the front right hand) is shown in the pose of bestowing grace. This conveys the idea that the

Lord bestows grace and protects all sincere devotees.

The colour gold symbolizes activity and thus the golden face of Brahma indicates that the Lord is active when involved in the process of creation. The white colour of the beard denotes wisdom and the length conveys the idea that creation is an eternal process. The crown on the head of the Lord implies that the Lord has supreme power and authority over the process of creation.

The lotus symbolizes the Supreme Reality, the essence of all things and beings in the universe. Brahma sitting or standing on a lotus indicates that he represents the creative power of the Supreme Reality. The colour white symbolizes

purity. Thus Brahma wearing clothes that are off-white, represents the dual nature of creation, that is purity and impurity, happiness and unhappiness, vice and virtue, knowledge and ignorance, and so on.

In Hindu mythology, a swan is said to possess a unique discriminating faculty, which enables it to distinguish pure milk from a mixture of milk and water. The swan is therefore used to symbolize the power of discrimination. Brahma uses the swan as a vehicle. This is intended to convey the idea that although creation is pluralistic in nature, there is only one Supreme Reality that the entire universe emanates from. This knowledge can be acquired by an individual by training his mind and intellect to acquire the power of right discrimination.

As creation is the work of the mind and the intellect, Lord Brahma symbolizes the Universal Mind. From the standpoint of an individual, Brahma symbolizes one's own mind and intellect. Since an individual is naturally gifted with the mind and intellect, he or she may be said to have already realized Brahma. For this reason also the worship of Brahma is not very popular. He is, however, worshipped by seekers of knowledge, such as students, teachers, scholars and scientists.

Jagat Shri Brahma Temple

Jagat Shri Brahma Temple, the only standing temple in India dedicated to Lord Brahma, the creator of the universe, is in Pushkar in Rajasthan. Pushkar is a small town on the edge of the Rajasthan desert. According to the Padma Purana, Brahma killed a demon with a lotus flower here. The lotus petals fell in three spots, where lakes emerged. As the *pushpa* (flower) fell from Brahma's *kar* (hand), so the place received the name Pushkar. The lakes are located within a radius of six miles. Senior Pushkar, where the hotels are located, is considered the most holy place, because the lotus fell here first. Middle Pushkar is 3 km down the road and has a small Hanuman temple and a 200 year old banyan tree. New (Junior) Pushkar, 3 km further north, has a small Krishna temple.

It is believed that to bathe in Pushkar Lake on Kartika Purima (the full moon day in Oct/Nov) gives one salvation. The full benefit of taking bath in Pushkar Lake is said to be during the last five days of Kartika month. Those who take bath at this time are said to be relieved of all sins and promoted to heaven when they leave their bodies. It is said to be especially auspicious to do *parikrama* (walk around) of the three Pushkars (16 km) on the Kartika Purnima. Gaya Kund, near Junior Pushkar, is where people do *puja* (worship) for the salvation of their ancestors.

As legend goes, at Pushkar, Brahma resolved to perform a sacred *yajna*. Brahma was to perform it with his wife Saraswati. At the appointed hour of the *yajna*, Saraswati was late as she was waiting for her companions. The hour was so auspicious that Brahma would not let the moment pass without the intended *yajna*. He therefore asked Indra to find a suitable girl for him to sit by his side as his wife for the *yajna*. Indra secured a girl called Gayatri. Brahma married her and kept his time. At this moment Saraswati came and saw Gayatri in her place and was highly enraged. Saraswati cursed Brahma by saying he would only be worshipped at Pushkar. Saraswati then went away to a hill, Rathkagir to the south of Pushkar where there is a temple dedicated to her.

Marble steps lead up to the Brahma temple where a silver turtle lies embossed in the floor facing the sanctorum. The marble floor around the turtle is littered with hundreds of silver coins embedded in the floor, and so are the walls of the temple. Images of the peacock, the vehicle of Brahma's consort Saraswati, adorn the temple walls. Brahma here is shown in a life-size form with four hands and four faces, facing four different directions. A *hans* (swan, the official carrier of Brahma) spans the gateway to the temple which is crowned with a red spire. Statues of Gayatri and Saraswati stand on left and right of Brahma's idol respectively.

Vishnu
Lord of Preservation

Vishnu is the Lord of protection, sustenance and maintenance. His consort Lakshmi is the possessor of wealth, which is necessary for maintenance. Goddess Lakshmi represents not only material wealth, but the wealth of valour, offspring, success, food, luxurious life and eternal bliss. Vishnu and Lakshmi thus help the souls introduced into the life cycle by Brahma to survive in the cycle of life.

Lord Vishnu represents the aspect of the Supreme Reality that preserves and sustains the universe. Although there are variations in images and pictures of Lord Vishnu, he is generally symbolized by a human body with four arms. In his hands he carries a conch (*shankha*), a mace (*gada*), and discus (*chakra*). He wears a crown, two earrings, a garland (*mala*) of flowers, and a red jewel around the neck. He has a blue body and wears yellow clothes (hence known as Pitambara). The Lord is shown reclining on a thousand-headed snake (named Ananta or Shesh Naag), and the snake stands with its hood open over the head of the Lord.

The four arms indicate Lord's omnipresence and omnipotence. A conch in the upper left hand indicates that the Lord communicates with his devotees with love and understanding. When blowing his conch, he reminds his devotees to live in this world with kindness and compassion towards all living beings. A *chakra* in his upper right hand conveys the idea that the Lord uses this weapon to protect his devotees from evil. The mace denotes energy and in the Lord's left lower hand signifies that he sustains the manifest world by the energy that he holds in himself. His lower right hand is depicted bestowing grace on his devotees.

The snake denotes the mind and the thousand heads of the snake signify innumerable desires and passions of an individual. Just as a snake destroys its victim by its venom, an uncontrolled mind destroys the world by the venom of its possessiveness. The Lord has controlled all desires, and this is symbolized by showing him seated or reclining on the coiled snake. When a sincere devotee of the Lord controls his desires, the Lord fulfills the devotee's genuine desires and helps him on his path.

The blue sky in the background of the Lord suggests that he pervades the entire universe. The blue colour symbolizes infinity. The blue body of the Lord signifies that he has infinite attributes. He is nameless, formless, and immeasurable. The colour yellow is associated with earthly existence and the yellow clothes of the Lord signify that he incarnates himself on this earth to uphold righteousness and destroy evil.

A flower garland around the Lord's neck is a symbol of the devotee's adoration for the Lord. A red jewel adorning his neck signifies that the Lord fulfills all genuine desires of his devotees and provides for their needs. The crown is a symbol

Divya Desams

It is considered that Azhwars were *amshams* (partial *avatara*) of Lord Sri Vishnu and they were sent by him to the earth to continue the good deeds that he had accomplished during his previous nine *avataras*. The Azhwars spent their time in constant chanting of the Lord in the knowledge that the Lord will grant them *moksha*. They were considered superior to the Rishis, because unlike the Rishis (who spent their times in forests in performing *yajnas*, to attain *moksha*), Azhwars spent their time among ordinary mortals and showed that even an ordinary person can follow the path towards *moksha* through their devotion.

To lead people to *moksha* through worship of the Lord, these Azhwars set forth to various holy sites in search of the places where Lord Sri Vishnu had come to this world. They identified 108 places as Divya Desams.

Among the 108 Divya Desams, it is believed that the following eight were self-manifested (not created by any human hands) known as Swayamvakta Kshetras. They are (1) Sri Rangam (2) Sri Mushnam (3) Tirumala (4) Shalagram (5) Naimisaranya (6) Thotadri (7) Pushkar (8) Badrinath.

of the Lord's supreme power and authority. The two earrings signify the dual nature of creation, such as knowledge and ignorance, happiness and unhappiness, and pleasure and pain.

Vishnu, preserver of human life is one of the three gods of the Trimurti. He is a generous god and known as being Sattvaguna (kind and merciful). Vishnu is the only god of the Trimurti who is reborn whenever there is a crisis on earth. According to the Puranas, if *dharma* (righteousness) is disturbed, Vishnu descends to earth as an *avatara* (a human form) to fight the forces of evil.

The Bhagavata, among other sources, say that there are twenty-two *avataras* of Vishnu. However, the widely accepted belief is that there are ten *avataras*, known as the Dashavatara. All the ten *avataras* are revered, but the seventh, Rama, and eighth, Krishna, are believed to be great heroes and worshipped as gods in their own right. Of Vishnu's *avataras*, the first four are believed to have occurred in the Krita Yuga, the fifth, sixth, and seventh in the Treta Yuga, the eighth in the Dwapara Yuga, and the ninth in the Kali Yuga. The tenth *avatara* has yet to appear, and it is believed that he will come at the end of the Kali Yuga.

Seen in order, the **Dashavatara** represents the evolution of mankind from the fish stage to *purusha* (man). These *avataras* were Matsya (fish), Kurma (tortoise), Varaha (boar), Narasimha (man-lion), Vamana (dwarf), Parashurama (a powerful warrior), Rama, Krishna, Buddha and Kalki (white horse).

Whenever Vishnu descends to earth he marries Lakshmi (his goddess wife). They are destined to marry on earth as in heaven. When Vishnu was Rama, Lakshmi was born as Sita. As Krishna he married her as Rukmini.

Vishnu Dashavatara

A great flood once threatened to submerge the earth. Manu, the ruler of the earth, in order to propitiate the gods, took a bowl of water to pray. In that bowl of water, appeared a fish who told Manu that if he looked after him, Manu would be saved from the flood. Manu agreed and took the fish to the ocean.

In the ocean Matsya, the fish, grew to whale-like proportions and taught Manu how to build a ship that could sail during the flood. While the deluge ripped the land apart and treacherous waves rose from the ocean, Manu was safe. Matsya was the tether who towed Manu's ship to safety. When they reached the shores they found a dead and barren land ravaged by the storm. Manu's cargo contained the seeds for every form of life, from which he could sow the world. Vishnu as Matsya supported Brahma who renewed the world.

There are several versions of the story in the Puranas of the way in which Vishnu assumed the aspect of a fish, so as to tow the ship in which Manu had taken refuge from the devastating flood. The same story is found in the Mahabharata, where the fish is described as having a horn, and in the Bhagavata Purana it is

further elaborated by the addition of a fight between Matsya and the demon Hayagriva (Horse-headed) who had stolen the Vedas while Brahma was asleep.

After the deluge, many cosmic treasures sank deep into the ocean. The *asuras* (demons) were in race against the *devas* (minor gods) to churn the oceans for *amrit* (the nectar of immortality).

Vishnu appeared as Kurma (tortoise) who sided with the *devas*. Together, they decided they would create a churn for obtaining the *amrit*. The serpent Vasuki was threaded around Mount Mandara to create a churn. Kurma dived to the floor of the ocean and balanced Mount Mandara on his back. In the grip of Kurma's cosmic force, Mount Mandara could not sink into the ocean

bed. The gods churned, and the nectar of immortality came into their hands.

As they continued to churn, fourteen treasures appeared. For Kurma the most precious was Lakshmi, the goddess of beauty and good fortune who would be his wife.

The other treasures were: Dhanvantari (physician of gods, who carried the pot which held the *amrit*), Sura (goddess of wine), Chandra (moon), Rambha (celestial nymph), Kaustubha (the precious gem for Vishnu's body), Uchchaihshravas (the divine horse, swift as thought), Parijata (wish-granting tree), Surabhi (wish-granting cow), Airavata (the four-tusked elephant), Panchajanya (conch shell), Sharanga (the invincible bow) and Visha (poison).

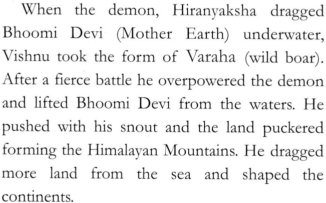

When the demon, Hiranyaksha dragged Bhoomi Devi (Mother Earth) underwater, Vishnu took the form of Varaha (wild boar). After a fierce battle he overpowered the demon and lifted Bhoomi Devi from the waters. He pushed with his snout and the land puckered forming the Himalayan Mountains. He dragged more land from the sea and shaped the continents.

Once a tyrannical demon king Hiranyakashipu tormented the world. He had the boon that he could not be slain either by man or beast, inside or outside the palace, by day or night. No god could overcome him and with each battle he won, the king's pride grew. Adopting the form of a lion-headed man, Narasimha, Vishnu approached the palace at dusk and hid in a pillar at the entrance out of which he sprang and killed the demon king Hiranyakashipu. Some sculptures show this incident taking place inside a pillar, and others show Narasimha with Hiranyakashipu on his lap tearing out his entrails.

Bali, the great-grandson of Hiranyakashipu was a virtuous and just monarch. His rule was so successful that his reputation began to overshadow that of Indra who was obliged to seek Vishnu's help in order to regain his supremacy. Not wishing to use harsh measures against such an exemplary ruler Vishnu resorted to a stratagem. He disguised himself as a Vamana (dwarf) and asked Bali to give him a piece of land three paces wide on which he could sit and meditate. Bali happily granted the request. Vishnu then used his supernatural powers to take possession of heaven and earth in two steps thus depriving Bali of his kingdom. Vamana's third step would have reached the lower world but Bali bowed before Vamana realising he had to be Vishnu. Pleased by Bali's humility, Vishnu spared him and gave Bali a

kingdom of his own in the netherworld. The image of Vamana holds a *kamandal* in his right hand and a staff in his left.

With the incarnation of Parashurama, there is a change from the type of mythology on which the preceding *avataras* were based. Most of the stories relating to the other five incarnations are on a superhuman plane whereas those about Parashurama usually have a worldlier element. The story behind the name and appearance of this *avatara* concerns sage Jamadagni's son, Rama, who became a brilliant archer. In gratitude for having this skill conferred on him he went to the Himalayas and worshipped Shiva for many years. Shiva was pleased with this devotion and, when war broke out between the gods and demons, ordered Rama to go and defeat the demons. Rama at that time was without his bow and he asked Shiva how he could comply without anything to fight with. Shiva assured him that if

he did as he was told he would conquer the demons and this Rama was able to do. As a reward, Shiva gave Rama many gifts and weapons; one of these was a magnificent axe (*parashu*) after which Rama was known as Parashurama (Rama with-the-axe). Vishnu, however, in another story had become his Parashurama incarnation for an entirely different reason. This was the result of a feud which had started because a king had stolen his father Jamadagni's wish-granting cow. Parashurama took his revenge for the theft by killing the king. In return the king's sons killed Parashurama's father. Vishnu took the form of Parashurama not only to get revenge but to rid the world of all oppression by kings, which he did in the course of 21 battles. Parashurama is the first incarnation in which Vishnu appears in a completely human form while at the same time keeping his status as a deity. His images are almost always two-handed and, hold an axe in their right hand.

The seventh incarnation of Lord Vishnu, Rama is said to have taken birth on earth to slay the demon Ravana and to annihilate the evil forces of the age. He is widely believed to be an actual historical figure whose exploits form the great Hindu epic Ramayana written by the ancient Sanskrit poet Valmiki. In the story of Ramayana, Rama's personality depicts him as the perfect son, devoted brother, true husband, trusted friend, ideal king, and a noble adversary. He was the eldest son of King Dasharatha, who ruled the kingdom of Ayodhya in north India. Early in his life, a sage called Vishwamitra recognised Rama as an *avatara* of Vishnu and sought his help in the slaying of demons. Right from adolescence, in his fight against evil, Rama was always victorious. This victory foreshadowed the great battle and slaying of Ravana, the demon king of Lanka. Rama is hardly different in looks from Lord Vishnu or Krishna. He is most often represented as a standing figure, with an arrow in his right hand, a bow in his left and a quiver on his back. A Rama statue is also usually accompanied by those of his wife Sita (Lakshmi's *avatara*), brother Lakshmana, and the legendary monkey attendant Hanuman. He is depicted in princely adornments with a *tilak* or mark on the forehead, and as having a dark, almost bluish complexion, which shows his relation with Vishnu. Rama's compassionate nature and his belief in duty elevated him as Maryada Purusha or ideal man. Two of India's greatest festive events - Dussehra commemorates the siege of Lanka and Rama's victory over Ravana; and Diwali, the festival of lights, celebrates Rama and Sita's homecoming to their kingdom in Ayodhya.

In his eighth *avatara*, Vishnu was Krishna the greatest teacher whose words form a priceless Hindu scripture, The Bhagwad Gita or the guide to life. Krishna was born on the eighth day of the holy month of Shravana in Mathura in North India. Kamsa, the demon had been warned that the eighth child of Devaki and Vasudev would bring about his doom. Kamsa imprisoned the pregnant Devaki along with Vasudev. The gods conspired; the child was taken to Yashoda and Nand, cowherds who lived in Vrindavan.

As a child, Krishna was mischievous, he had a taste for butter and was affectionately called Makhan Chor (butter thief). His childhood playmates were *gopas* (cowherd boys) and *gopis* (cowherd girls), who were greatly devoted to him. Of all *gopis*, Radha loved Krishna the most. In the forests of Vrindavan, Krishna often played his flute and *gopis* danced with him in ecstasy. The *gopis* represent the individual souls trapped in physical bodies. Radha symbolizes the individual soul that is awakened to the love of God and is absorbed in such love. The sound of Krishna's flute represents the call of the Divine for the individual souls. The dance of the *gopis* and Krishna (Rasa Lila) signifies the union of the human and Divine, the dance of the souls.

Krishna married Rukmini, an incarnation of Lakshmi. Rukmini's brother had promised her hand in marriage to Shishupal, an incarnation of Ravana. On their wedding day she eloped with Krishna. But before they could

marry, Krishna had to kill the demons Shishupal and Jarasandha.

As his charioteer, on the battlefield of Kurukshetra, Krishna was the first to see Arjuna overcome by the realisation that he would cause the death of his gurus and relatives. While the armies of the Pandavas and the Kauravas stood facing each other with their arrows drawn, Krishna, recited the Bhagwad Gita, the nucleus of Hindu philosophy. While every turn in his life is marked by a battle against evil, Krishna is most respected for Bhagawad Gita. Of all the incarnations, Lord Krishna is revered as a full and complete incarnation (*purna avatara*) of Lord Vishnu.

As Buddha, Vishnu was a great religious teacher of India. Gautama, the Buddha was born in 544 BC in Lumbini, Nepal. Saddened by the realization that life was a meaningless and hollow passage from one state of being to the next, the prince went into deep meditation under a Bodhi tree near Gaya, until he finally attained enlightenment, on the full moon day of Vaishakh. He thereafter became known as the Buddha. The Buddha, reached Nirvana or the extinction of self and freedom from the cycle of rebirth, also on the full moon day of Vaishakh.

Vishnu's final *avatara* will be as Kalki. At the end of the present age (Kali Yuga) he will come riding a white horse. Predictions say Kalki will be brandishing a flaming sword and will destroy all evil on earth, after which purity will reign, once again in another Treta Yuga.

Badrinath

Cradled in the twin Himalayan Mountain ranges of Nar and Narayan is Badrinath, on the bank of river Alaknanda in Uttaranchal. With Neelkanth Mountains as the backdrop, the shrine is dedicated to Vishnu. The present temple was built about two centuries ago by the Garhwal Kings. There are 15 idols in the temple complex, each sculpted in black stone. The principal idol represents Vishnu in a meditative posture and is flanked by Nara-Narayan. Legend dates it prior to the Vedic age though it is believed to have been re-established by Adi Shankaracharya, in 8th century AD. Some of the other images include Lakshmi (Vishnu's consort), Garuda (Vishnu's mount), Shiva, Parvati and Ganesha.

Besides the main temple of Badrinath there are four other smaller Badri temples. These are collectively called the Panch Badris or five Badris.

- *Yogadhyan Badri*
  Closest to the main temple of Badrinath lies the tiny, sleepy hamlet of Pandukeshwar, which is the winter home for the idol at Badrinath. It is believed that King Pandu, father of Pandavas, installed a bronze statue called Yogadhyan Badri. Some years ago, four ancient metal foils engraved with a description of several kings in the region were discovered here. Believed to be over 1500 years old, these foils are kept at Joshimath, 30 km downstream.

- *Bhavishya Badri*
  The bhavishya or future Badri is situated at Subain near Tapovan, about 20 km east of Joshimath. According to Hindu belief, when evil is on the rise in this world, the two mountains Nara and Narayan at Badrinath will close up on each other and destroy the route to the present Badrinath. This would also mark the end of the present world and the beginning of a new one. Lord Badrinath will then appear at the Bhavishya Badri temple and be worshipped here instead of at the present one.

- *Vridha Badri*
  Vridha Badri or the old Badri is the third temple, in a village called Animath, near Joshimath, on the main Rishikesh-Badrinath motor road. Legend says that when rishi Narada did tapasya here, lord Vishnu appeared. It is believed that Badrinath was worshipped here before his enshrinement by Shankaracharya at the main Badrinath seat. The temple of Vridha Badri is open throughout the year.

- *Adi Badri*
  Adi Badri is the farthest from the other four Badris. It is approachable from Karnaprayag by a motorable road enroute Ranikhet. The temple complex has 16 small temples with intricate carvings. Seven of these temples belong to the late Gupta period. Local tradition assigns these buildings to Shankaracharya. The main temple is distinguished by a pyramid shaped raised platform, with a black stone idol of Vishnu.

Shiva
Lord of Destruction

Shiva is known as the destroyer in the Trimurti. He has a 1,008 names, including Mahadeva (the great god), Mahesh, Rudra, Neelkantha (the blue-throated one), and Ishwar (the supreme god). He is also called Mahayogi, or the great ascetic, who symbolises the highest form of austere penance and abstract meditation, which results in salvation.

The name Shiva does not appear in the Vedas. However he is identified with the Vedic god Rudra, lord of songs, sacrifice, nourishment, the healer of diseases and provider of property. Shiva is said to have five faces, corresponding to his five tasks, the *panchakriya*: creation, establishment, destruction, oblivion, and grace. His five faces are associated with the creation of the sacred syllable Om.

Shiva is said to live on Mount Kailash, in the Himalayas. His vehicle is Nandi the bull and his weapon, the *trishul*. Shiva's consort is Parvati, who is also believed to be a part of Shiva. One of the most popular forms of Shiva is that of Ardhanarishvara. According to a story in the Puranas, Brahma was unsuccessful at creation.

He propitiated Shiva who took this form and separated Parvati from his body. Parvati has many incarnations, like Kali, Durga, and Uma. Their sons are Kartikeya and Ganesha. Shiva is believed to have a large number of attendants, called *ganas*. These mythological beings have human bodies with animal heads. Shiva's son Ganesha is the leader of the *ganas*.

The Linga Purana says that Brahma and Vishnu were once arguing over who was the supreme being. Suddenly, there appeared before them a huge column of fire. Both of them decided to find one end each. Whoever returned first would be acknowledged as supreme. Vishnu assumed the form of a boar and dug into the earth, Brahma in the form of a swan, flew upwards. They searched for days but in vain. Then Shiva appeared in the fiery column. Brahma and Vishnu realised their mistake and acknowledged Shiva as the Supreme Being. The Shivalinga represents that column of fire.

Shivalingas worshipped in temples are mostly made of stone and consist of three parts. The lowest portion in the shape of a square

symbolises Brahma (the Lord of Creation). The middle part in the shape of an octagon symbolises Vishnu (the Lord of Preservation). These two portions are embedded inside a pedestal. The cylindrical portion projecting from the pedestal symbolises Shiva (the Lord of Destruction).

Since the tasks of Lord Shiva are numerous, He cannot be symbolized in one form. For this reason the images of Shiva vary significantly in their symbolism. Images of Shiva in his physical form present him as a soothing meditative figure. His unclad body is covered with ashes. The unclad body symbolizes the transcendental aspect of the Lord. Since all things reduce to

ashes when burned, ashes symbolize the physical universe. The ashes on the unclad body of the Lord signify that Shiva is the source of the entire universe, but he transcends the physical phenomena and is not affected by it. Lord Shiva is the master of yoga. The matted locks on the head of the Lord convey the integration of the physical, mental and spiritual energies in yoga.

His ornaments are not gold and precious stones. He wears a snake Vasuki around his neck. He is also known as Neelkantha (blue-throated), for he holds Vasuki's poison in his throat. The legend dates back to the time when the gods churned the oceans. Vasuki's poison threatened the world. Only Shiva could take the poison in his

mouth. He held it in his throat forever and earned the name Neelkantha. Vasuki Naga is shown curled three times around the neck of the Lord and is looking towards his right side. The three coils of the snake symbolize the past, present and future - time in cycles. The Lord wearing the curled snake like an ornament signifies that creation proceeds in cycles and is time dependent, but the Lord himself transcends time. The right side of the body symbolizes the human activities based upon knowledge, reason and logic. The snake looking towards the right side of the Lord signifies that the Lord's eternal laws of reason and justice preserve natural order in the universe. Rudra is another name of Shiva. Rudra also means 'strict or uncompromising' and *aksha*

means eye. Rudraksha necklace worn by the Lord illustrates that he uses his cosmic laws firmly - without compromise - to maintain law and order in the universe. The necklace has 108 beads which symbolize the elements used in the creation of the world. He wears a pair of unmatched earrings that symbolise his being Ardhanarishvara (half man and half woman). One earring is a Kundala, worn by men and the other a Tatanka worn by women. The crescent moon adorns his crown, signifying his control on the time cycle.

Also known as Pashupati, Lord of the animals, Shiva sits on a tiger skin subduing aggression. One hand is raised in the *abhaya-mudra*, for he is the benevolent force of destruction. He has a

third eye on his forehead which is the source of knowledge and wisdom. The holy Ganga imprisoned in his flowing locks signifies that the Lord destroys sin, removes ignorance, and bestows knowledge, purity and peace on the devotees. In his two arms Shiva holds the *trishul* (the three prongs representing the three *gunas* of *sattva, tamas* and *rajas*) in one and *damaru* (a small drum symbolising creative activity) in the other. His *vahana* is the Nandi, the bull. The bull symbolizes both power and ignorance. Lord Shiva's use of the bull as a vehicle conveys the idea that he removes ignorance and bestows power of wisdom on his devotees.

Shiva sitting in the cremation ground signifies that he is the controller of death in the physical world. Since birth and death are cyclic, controlling one implies controlling the other. Thus, Lord Shiva is revered as the ultimate controller of birth and death.

The above description should convey him as an angry and destructive image, yet being the source of all knowledge he is often in a meditative pose with half closed eyes looking out into the universe as well as into his inner self, signifying that his act of destruction is in itself an act of creation for in the absence of destruction there can be no creation.

Historically, Shiva reveals himself in secular as well as religious texts. A Dravidian king he married Sati a daughter of an Aryan king. Sati's father, Daksha opposed their union. After the wedding, at a *yajna* (sacrifice), being performed by Daksha. Shiva was ignored by his father-in-law who found him 'uncivilised'. Sati couldn't bear this humiliation of her husband, and jumped into the sacrificial fire. When Shiva came to collect her ashes he could only express his deep pain and grief through a violent dance called the Tandava. He terrified all creation as he danced around the earth seven times.

When nothing would pacify Shiva, the gods feared his sorrow could destroy the earth. They decided to revive Sati and she was born as Parvati (daughter of the mountains).

Meanwhile, Shiva had renounced the world and gone to Mount Kailash where he had begun a harsh penance. When Parvati reached Mount Kailash, Shiva was so involved in his meditation that he was immune to Parvati's presence. Parvati did all she could to entice Shiva but his meditation was powerful. Finally she asked Madan/Kama (the god of love) for help. Kama told her to dance in front of Shiva. When Parvati danced, Madan shot an arrow laced with flowers at Shiva, whose penance broke. When Shiva opened his eyes, his first sight was Parvati dancing before him. Shiva fell in love with Parvati and became her loving husband. Parvati became his *shakti* (creative force).

Shiva once granted a peculiar boon to a demon called Bhasmasura, who wished that if he placed his hand on anyone's head, that person would turn to ashes. No sooner was his wish granted than he menaced Shiva himself, who took to his heels and was saved by Vishnu, in the form of Mohini, the enchantress. Induced by Mohini to join her dance, the

demon soon killed himself by placing his hand on his own head. Shiva and Mohini combined their energies and produced Hari-Hara *putra* (Vishnu-Shiva's son), later identified with Sasta or Aiyappa, a celibate tribal deity in Kerala. He lives on in Mohiniattam, the feminine counterpart of Kerala's classical dance form, Kathakali.

Shiva is the creator of dance and of the first 16 rhythmic syllables ever uttered, from which the Sanskrit language was born. His dance of anger is called the Raudra Tandava and his dance of joy, the Ananda Tandava. All the gods and sages were present when he first danced the Nadanta Tandava, a characteristically vigorous dance, and they begged him to dance again. Shiva promised to do so in the hearts of his

devotees and in a sacred grove in Tamil Nadu, where the great temple of Chidambaram was built, the only one in India dedicated to Shiva as Nataraja, the lord of dance. It is believed that on the 13th day of each bright lunar fortnight, after 6 o'clock in the evening, falls a sacred hour called Pradosha. Worshipping Shiva at this time is akin to worshipping all the powers of the universe, for this is the time when all the gods are believed to have assembled on Kailash to lose themselves in the ecstasy of Nataraja's dance.

Lord Shiva is the Lord of mercy and compassion. He protects devotees from evil forces such as lust, greed, and anger. He grants boons, bestows grace and awakens wisdom in his devotees.

Dwadasa Jyotirlingam

The Dwadasa Jyotirlingam shrines or the 12 shrines enshrining Shiva in the form of a Jyotirlingam, have been held in reverence since time immemorial in the Indian system of beliefs. The southernmost of these is located at Rameswaram, while the northernmost is located in the snowy heights of the Himalayas at Kedarnath. These temples are closely linked with legends from the Puranas and are rich in history and tradition.

Somnath is the foremost of the 12 Jyotirlingam shrines of Shiva, held in reverence throughout India and is rich in legend, tradition and history. It is located at Prabhas Patan in Saurashtra in Gujarat.

Mallikarjuna is enshrined in Sree Sailam near Kurnool, an ancient temple rich in architectural and sculptural wealth. Adi Sankaracharya composed his Sivanandalahiri here.

Mahakaleshwar Jyotirlingam shrine is in the ancient and historic city of Ujjain or Avanti in Madhya Pradesh.

Omkareshwar Jyotirlingam shrine is on an island in the course of the river Narmada in Madhya Pradesh, and is also home to the Amareshwar temple.

Kedarnath the northernmost of the Jyotirlingams, nestled in the snow clad Himalayas in Uttaranchal, is an ancient shrine rich in legend and tradition. It is accessible only on foot, six months in a year.

Bhimashankar is associated with the legend of Shiva destroying the demon Tripurasura. The shrine is located in the Sahyadri hills of Maharashtra, accessed from Pune.

Vishwanath Jyotirlingam shrine in Varanasi, Uttar Pradesh, is the most celebrated pilgrimage site in India. It is the goal of thousands of pilgrims that visit this ancient city.

Tryambakeshwar Jyotirlingam shrine is intimately linked with the origin of the river Godavari, near Nashik in Maharashtra.

Vaidyanath shrine is located at Deogarh. The ancient pilgrimage town of Deogarh is in the Santal Parganas area of Bihar

Nageshwar near Dwarka in Gujarat is one of the most popular shrines of Shiva.

Rameswara or *Ramalingeswara* is the southernmost Jyotirlingam shrine of India. This vast temple is on the island of Rameswaram, in southern Tamil Nadu.

Grishneshwar Jyotirlingam shrine is located in the vicinity of the tourist town of Ellora in Maharashtra, which has several rock-cut caves from the 1st millennium CE.

Hanuman

the Monkey-God

Hanuman or Anjaneya or Kesarinandan is the son of Anjana Devi and Kesari. Anjana was once a celestial maiden and was born as a monkey-woman as a result of a curse. When the king of Ayodhya, Dasharatha performed a *yajna* praying for a son, he was yielded a bowl of *payasam* or *kheer* from the fire. His wives shared the *prasada* and thus Rama, Lakshmana, Bharata and Shatrughana were born. A portion of this *payasam* was carried away by the lord of winds, Vayu Deva and fell in the hands of Anjana Devi and she gave birth to Hanuman. That is why Hanuman is also known as Maruti or Pavanputra or the son of Vayu.

He grew up as strong and mischievous. He could travel as fast as the wind. He once mistook the glowing sun to be a fruit and flew up to the sky to reach for it. Lord Indra was upset and struck Anjaneya with his thunderbolt. Vayu Deva was upset that his son was struck and stopped blowing. The whole world was in trouble without the winds. All the gods offered various powerful boons to Anjaneya, thus making him more powerful and invincible than

before. Vayu Deva was pleased and resumed his work. Anjaneya was once causing trouble to the rishis, not really realising the might of his playful actions. The angry rishis cursed him that he would cease to realise and recognise his powers unless someone reminded him of it. This calmed him down and he started his

lessons with the rishis. Then the mighty Hanuman travelled with Surya at his speed and mastered all the scriptures.

He played a major role in Ramayana, the great epic by Valmiki. When Rama was banished from his kingdom Ayodhya by his step-mother Kaikeyi, he reached the forest with his wife Sita and brother Lakshmana. Sugreeva and his army with Hanuman as the commander-in-chief were hiding from Sugreeva's brother Vaali. Rama helped Sugreeva in defeating his brother and winning his kingdom back. In gratitude, Sugreeva deployed his monkey-army in the service of Rama. Sita was abducted by the demon-king Ravana and imprisoned in Lanka, his kingdom an island off the southern tip of India. Brandishing his mace, Hanuman took a single leap across the

gulf separating the two countries and located Sita. The demons of Lanka tried to capture Hanuman. They set fire to his tail, hoping to scare him; but Hanuman turned his tail on the city and set Lanka on fire. When Lakshmana was wounded, Hanuman flew to the Himalayas for the medicinal herb Sanjeevani. Unable to identify it, he picked up the entire mountain and carried it to Lakshmana. When the victorious Rama returned to Ayodhya and was crowned king, Hanuman continued to serve him, ever at his service.

After his coronation, following the victory in the battle with Ravana, Rama distributed gifts to all those who had assisted him in his battle with Ravana. Turning towards Hanuman, Rama said, "There is nothing I can give you that would match the service you have rendered to me. All I can do

is to give you my own self." Upon hearing these words, Hanuman stood by Rama, in all humility, with hands joined together and head slightly bent in the pose of service. To this day, this picture of Hanuman, as a humble devotee of the Lord, is the most popular among the admirers and worshippers of Hanuman.

He featured in the other epic Mahabharata as well. He stood by the Pandavas in the Kurukshetra war. He stabilised and protected Arjuna's chariot by being present in the flag flying on the chariot. He was thus honoured with witnessing the Gita-*upadesh* firsthand.

He is worshipped in the temples as Bhakta Hanuman and Veera Hanuman. There are also separate temples for Hanuman. As Bhakta Hanuman, he is seen holding both hands together in prayer. He is seen as Veera Hanuman, holding the mace in one hand and the Sanjeevani *parvat* in the other. The worship of Hanuman, therefore, symbolizes the worship of the Supreme Lord, for acquiring knowledge, physical and mental strength, truthfulness, sincerity, selflessness, humility, loyalty, and profound devotion to the Lord.

Hanuman symbolically stands as the mental body in a human being. The mind is fickle (like a monkey) and jumps from place to place, going after things, engaging itself in innumerable activities that disturb the peace of the place. The mind, like Hanuman can also travel where it wants to. It can fly in the air, cross the continents and the worlds in an instant and

reach any one and anything it wants to mentally. It can also expand or contract itself at will (again like Hanuman). So long as it remains under the control of pure animal passions and the activities of the senses, it remains unstable and mischievous, causing a lot of disturbance in the world of the individual. But once it surrenders to the inner self (Lord Rama) and becomes devoted to it completely and unconditionally, it assumes miraculous powers and performs stupendous feats. By killing all the evil thoughts with its determination, it also lays a firm foundation for the kingdom of God (Ramarajya) to become established in the body. Hanuman is thus symbolically the mind principle ever absorbed in the contemplation of God and totally surrendered to Him.

As Bajarangbali, he is strong in both devotion and physical strength. He is an ocean of virtues and friend of the pure hearted. He loves the ascetic qualities in man because only those who are detached and mentally free from the luxuries of life and desires of their bodies can truly concentrate on the Divine and attain Him.

Hanuman is regarded as the superman, the knowledge body (*gyana guna sagara*) in man, the immortal man (*chiranjeevi*) and also the animal man (*va-nara*). He is a perfect example of true devotion and complete surrender. He also symbolizes the story of animal man in us who through the path of devotion and service to God, can purify himself and attain immortality.

India has innumerable Anjaneya (Hanuman) temples

1. Sri Veera Anjaneya Temple of Mylapore, Chennai, Tamil Nadu
2. Sri Veera Mangala Anjaneya Temple, Nallatore, Tamil Nadu
3. Sri Yoga Anjaneya Temple, Solingar, Tamil Nadu
4. Sri Pracheen Hanuman Mandir of New Delhi
5. Sri Digambara temple of Hanuman at Sidhabari, Himachal Pradesh
6. Sri Viswaroopa Anjaneya Swamy at Nerul, Navi Mumbai, Maharashtra
7. Sri Jaya Veera Anjaneya Swamy at Tanjavur, Tamil Nadu
8. Sri Jakhoo Hanuman Mandir, Simla, Himachal Pradesh
9. Sri Mukhya Praana (Anjaneya) Temple of Triplicane, Chennai, Tamil Nadu
10. Sri Sitarama Dasa Anjaneya Temple of Dharmapuri, Tamil Nadu
11. Sri Karanji Anjaneya Temple of Basavangudi, Bangalore, Karnataka
12. Sri Veera Anjaneya Temple of Chengalput, Tamil Nadu
13. Sri Sanjeevirayan Temple of Iyenkulam, Kanchipuram, Tamil Nadu
14. Sri Veera Anjaneya Temple of Ananthamangalam, Tamil Nadu
15. Sri Hanuman Ambalam of Alathoor, Malappuram, Kerala
16. Sri Anjaneya of Namakkal Digambara Temple, Tamil Nadu
17. Sri Dasanjaneya of Machavaram, Vijayawada, Andhra Pradesh
18. Sri Anjaneya of Haumarambalam, Payyanur, Kerala
19. Sri Jaya Anjaneya of Lalapet, Karur, Tamil Nadu
20. Sri Mahavir Temple, Sirulee, Puri, Orissa
21. Sri Kallukuzi Anjaneya Temple of Trichy, Tamil Nadu
22. Sri Panki Hanuman Temple of Panki, Kanpur, Uttar Pradesh
23. Sri Veera Anjaneya Temple of Cuddalore, Tamil Nadu
24. Sri Hanuman Badi Temple (Old) of Aliganj, Lucknow, Uttar Pradesh
25. Sri Hanuman Badi Temple (New) of Aliganj of Lucknow, Uttar Pradesh
26. Sri Hanuman Garhi, Nainital, Uttaranchal
27. Sri Anuvavi Anjaneya Temple, Coimbatore, Tamil Nadu
28. Sri Kote Anjaneya Temple, Palaghat, Kerala
29. Sri Nettikanti Anjaneya Temple, Kasapuram, Andhra Pradesh
30. Sri Anjaneya Swamy Temple near Nalu Kal Mandap in Tanjavur, Tamil Nadu

Ganesha

Lord Who Removes Obstacles

 Ganesha is the most widely worshipped Hindu God, a deity in a human form but with the head of an elephant, representing the power of the Supreme Being that removes obstacles and ensures success in human endeavours. For this reason, Hindus worship Ganesha first before beginning any religious, spiritual or worldly activity. As he is considered to be the Lord who removes obstacles (*vighnam*), he is also called Vighneshwara

In Hindu mythology, Lord Ganesha is the son of Lord Shiva and the Divine Mother Parvati. The portrayal of Lord Ganesha as the blend of human and animal parts symbolizes the ideals of perfection as conceived by Hindu sages and illustrates some philosophical concepts of profound spiritual significance.

The large head of an elephant symbolizes wisdom, understanding, and a discriminating intellect that one must possess to attain perfection in life. The wide mouth represents the natural human desire to enjoy life in the world. The large ears signify that a perfect person is the one who possesses a great capacity to listen to others and assimilate ideas. There is no known human instrument that has an operating range as wide as that of an elephant's trunk. It can uproot a tree and yet lift a needle off the ground. Likewise, the human mind must be strong enough to face the ups and downs of the external world and yet be delicate enough to

explore the subtle realms of the inner world. The two tusks denote the two aspects of the human personality, wisdom and emotion. The right tusk represents wisdom and the left tusk represents emotion. The broken left tusk conveys the idea that one must conquer emotions with wisdom to attain perfection.

The elephant eyes are said to possess natural deceptiveness that allows them to perceive objects to be bigger than what they really are. Thus the elephant eyes symbolize the idea that even if an individual gets bigger and bigger in wealth and wisdom, he should perceive others to be bigger than himself; that is, surrender one's pride and attain humility. The four arms indicate that the Lord is omnipresent and omnipotent. The left side of the body symbolizes emotion and the right side symbolizes reason. An axe in the upper left hand and a lotus in the upper right hand signify that in order to attain spiritual perfection, one should cut worldly attachments and conquer emotions. This enables one to live in the world without being affected by earthly temptations, just as a lotus remains in water but is not affected by it. A tray of *laddus* (sweets) near the Lord denotes that he bestows wealth and prosperity upon his devotees. The lower right hand is shown in a blessing pose, which signifies that Ganesha always blesses his devotees. The right foot dangling over the left foot illustrates that in order to live a successful life one should utilize knowledge and reason to overcome emotions.

Ganesha's body is usually portrayed wearing red and yellow clothes. Yellow symbolizes purity, peace and truthfulness. Red symbolizes the activity in the world. These are the qualities of a perfect person who performs all duties in the world, with purity, peace, and truthfulness. The big belly signifies that a perfect individual must have a large capacity to face all pleasant and unpleasant experiences of the world.

A mouse symbolizes the ego that can nibble all that is good and noble in a person. A mouse sitting near the feet of Ganesha indicates that a perfect person is one who has conquered his (or her) ego. A mouse gazing at the *laddus*, but not consuming them, denotes that a purified or controlled ego can live in the world without being affected by the worldly temptations. The mouse is also the vehicle of Ganesha, signifying that one must control ego in order for wisdom to shine forth.

His trunk is twisted into an embodiment of 'Om', the syllable that created the world. To combat evil, he carries weapons: discus, trident, sword and axe. A broken tusk is a reminder of his battle with a demon, and the fight with the forces of evil. Yet, the same tusk is used by him in the writing of the epic, the Mahabharata. When Vyasa wanted to compose the Mahabharata, Brahma suggested Ganesha be his scribe. Vyasa agreed and Ganesha used his broken tusk as a writing quill. Vyasa dictated the entire epic in verse and Ganesha recorded every word.

He is considered a bachelor, but according to another school of thought, he has two Shaktis - Siddhi and Riddhi. Siddhi represents success and prosperity. Riddhi represents wisdom.

In myths, the birth of Ganesha is celebrated as a divine twist of fate. A popular myth brings alive

the story about the elephant head. It all began when Parvati, wanted to bathe. She needed privacy and since there was no one at hand, she created a boy with the *ubtan* (paste of herbs) and oils from her body. She brought the figure to !ife and told him to stand guard while she bathed.

When Shiva, her husband, returned home; he found his way blocked by an unknown person. The guard blocked Shiva's entry, making him furious, and a duel began. The boy fought well, but was no match against the might of Shiva, who killed him. Parvati came out and saw the dead boy; she demanded he be brought back to life. Shiva sent his *ganas* to collect the head of the first living being, who was sleeping with head facing north. The north was associated with wisdom. Airavat, Indra's white elephant paid the price for Shiva's blunder. While Airavat slept facing the north, Shiva's *ganas* beheaded him. His head was carried away for the dead boy. An incensed Parvati demanded that her child be promoted to the status of a primary god. Shiva and all the other gods knew this was the only way they could placate her and Ganesha took his place before all the gods.

Another legend, explains Ganesha's role in changing astronomy. In the month of Shravan/Bhadrapad, after a feast of *laddus* Ganesha was on his way home. He was riding his mouse, a snake slithered into their path, the mouse tripped and Ganesha took a tumble. His stomach split, and the *laddus* fell out, Chandra (the moon) was watching and began to laugh. Ganesha picked up the snake and used it as a belt to hold his stomach together. He looked

up, cursed Chandra and banned him from the night skies.

Soon the gods and humankind were dazed by glare of the relentless sun. There was no respite of darkness when the moon was banished from the sky. The gods took a delegation to Ganesha and pleaded their case. Ganesha gave in, but made an astronomic condition. The moon would never shine like before. Full moon would be just once a month (earlier every day was a full moon). On other days the Chandra, as a reminder of his misdemeanour, would wax or wane.

Ganesha temples are seen in almost every village in India. Chubby and gleeful elephant headed Ganesha easily finds his place in the hearts of gods and people.

Forms of Ganesha

Baala Ganapati : Red coloured image of a four armed Ganesha

Dharuna Vinayaka : Red coloured image of an eight armed Ganesha

Bhakti Vinayaka ; Grey coloured image of four armed Ganesha

Veera Vinayaka : Red coloured image of sixteen armed Ganesha

Shakti Ganapati : Red coloured image of four armed Ganesha, seated with his consort to his left

Dwija Vinayaka : White coloured image of four faced Ganesha with four arms

Siddhi Vinayaka : Golden coloured image of four armed Ganesha

Ucchishta Ganapati : Blue coloured image of six armed Ganesha with his consort

Vighna Vinayaka : Gold coloured image of eight armed Ganesha

Kshipra Ganapati : Red coloured image of four armed Ganesha bearing a *ratna kumbham*

Heramba Vinayaka : Black image of ten armed Ganesha with five faces, seated on a lion

Lakshmi Vinayaka : White coloured image of eight armed Ganesha with two consorts

Makara Vinayaka : Red coloured image of Ganesha with a third eye, ten arms, bearing a *ratna kumbham*, with his consort

Vijaya Vinayaka : Red coloured image of four armed Ganesha on the *mooshaka* mount

Nritta Vinayaka : Gold coloured image of Ganesha in a dancing posture

Urdhva Vinayaka : Gold coloured image of six armed Ganesha with his consort

Ekakshara Vinayaka : Red coloured image of Ganesha with a third eye, seated on a lotus

Vara Vinayaka : Red coloured image of four armed Ganesha with a third eye

Dhryakshara Vinayaka : Gold image of four armed Ganesha, decorated with ear rings

Kshipraprasaada Vinayaka : Red coloured image of six armed Ganesha

Haridra Vinayaka : Yellow coloured image of four armed Ganesha

Ekadanta Vinayaka : Blue coloured image of four armed Ganesha

Srishti Vinayaka : Red coloured image of four armed Ganesha seated on his *mooshaka* mount

Utthanda Vinayaka : Red coloured image of ten armed Ganesha with his consort to his left

Ranamochana Vinayaka : Crystal image of four armed Ganesha

Dundi Vinayaka : Four armed Ganesha bearing a tusk, garland, axe and *ratna kumbham*

Dwimukha Vinayaka : Red coloured image of Ganesha with two faces and four arms

Trimukha Vinayaka : Red Ganesha with three faces and six arms seated on a golden lotus

Simha Vinayaka : White coloured image of Ganesha with eight arms
(One arm bearing a lion's face)

Yoga Vinayaka : Red coloured image of Ganesha in the posture of a yogi

Durga Vinayaka : Red coloured image of Ganesha with eight arms

Sankatahara Vinayaka : Red coloured image of four armed Ganesha clothed in blue, seated on a lotus *peetham* with his consort to his left

Devi

The Rig Veda contemplated the universe as the result of an interplay between the male principle (*purusha*), the prime source of generative power but dormant, and a female principle (*prakriti*), an active principle that manifests power (*shakti*) at work in the world.

Parvati, in a variety of forms, is the most common focus of devotion in India. She presents two main facets to her worshippers: a benign and accepting personality that provides assistance and a powerful and dangerous personality that must be placated.

The goddess Durga is a great warrior who carries a sword and a shield, rides a tiger, and destroys demons when the gods prove incapable; in this incarnation, she never submits, but remains capable of terrible deeds of war. The goddess Kali often appears as an even more horrific vision of the divine, with garlands of human skulls around her neck and a severed head in her hand; her bloody tongue hangs from her mouth and the weapons in her arms drip gore. This image attempts to capture the destructive capacity of the Divine, the suffering in the world, and the ultimate return of all things back to the Divine.

In many small shrines throughout India, the female divinity receives regular gifts of blood sacrifices, usually chickens and goats. Many more localized forms of goddesses, known by different names in different regions, are the focus for prayers and vows that lead worshipers to undertake acts of austerity and pilgrimages in return for favours. In addition, the goddess may manifest herself as the bearer of a number of diseases. The goddess of smallpox, known as Shitala in North India and Mariamman in South India, remains a feared and worshiped figure even after the official elimination of the disease, for she is still capable of afflicting people with a number of fevers and poxes.

Uma

Kurma Purana has an account of Uma's creation which takes us back, a stage before her birth as a daughter of Daksha. When Brahma was angry with his sons for adopting an ascetic life and refusing to perpetuate the human race, a form half male and half female was produced from that anger, to whom Brahma said, "Divide thyself," and then disappeared. The male half became Rudra or Shiva, and the female, Shakti or Devi.

Uma is the name by which the consort of Shiva is first known. When Devi (the goddess) appears as Uma, she is said to be the daughter of Daksha, a son of Brahma. As Shiva is called Mahadeva, Uma is frequently called simply Devi. At this period of her existence she is also called Sati, in allusion to the fact that when her father slighted her husband by not inviting him to the great sacrifice he made, she voluntarily entered the sacrificial fire and was burned to death in the presence of all the gods and brahmins. The name Sati means the true or virtuous woman. Ambika, another name of Uma, is said to be the wife of Rudra. As in Shiva, Agni and Rudra are combined, so too his wife is regarded as a compound of several divine forms. Uma, Ambika, Parvati, Haimavati are the names belonging to the wife of Rudra, others as Kali to the wife of Agni.

Parvati

The goddess Parvati is the constant companion of her husband Shiva, and the mother of Kartikeya and Ganesha, but few independent actions are ascribed to her. In the Puranas, Shiva and Parvati are generally represented as engaged in making love to each other or as seated on Mount Kailash discussing Hindu philosophy. Occasionally, however, quarrels arose between them, and on one such occasion Shiva reproached her for the darkness of her complexion. This taunt so grieved her that she left him and went to a deep forest to perform severe course of austerities, until Brahma granted her a boon that her complexion be golden, and she was known as Gauri.

Varaha Purana describes her origin. Once Brahma, Vishnu and Shiva met at Mount Kailash to solve the problem of a mighty *asura* named Andhaka, who was troubling all the gods. As the three deities looked at each other, from their three refulgent glances sprang into being a virgin of celestial loveliness in three colours, white, red and black. Brahma then praising her, said, "Thou shalt be named the goddess of three times (past,

present and future), the preserver of the universe, and under various appellations shalt thou be worshipped, as thou shalt be the cause of accomplishing the desires of thy votaries. But, O goddess, divide thyself into three forms, according to the colours by which thou art

distinguished." She then divided herself into three parts, one white, one red, and one black. The white was Saraswati of a lovely felicitous form, and the consort of Brahma in creation; the red was Lakshmi, the beloved of Vishnu and the black was Parvati, endowed with many qualities and the energy of Shiva.

The Vaivarta Purana relates the circumstance which led to the re-appearance on earth of Uma, who had sacrificed herself and became a Sati, in the form of Parvati.

Shiva, hearing of the death of his wife, fainted from grief. Brahma and Vishnu were very upset to see this. Vishnu promised Shiva that he would get her consort back in another form, since Shiva and Sati were as inseparable as cold from water, heat from fire, smell from earth, or radiance from the sun.

Not long after this, Sati was born as Parvati, the daughter of Mena, Himavat's wife. Whilst still a girl, she heard a voice from heaven saying, "Perform severe austerities, in order to obtain Shiva for a husband, as he cannot otherwise be obtained." She had to perform most severe penance before she was reunited to her husband; and it was only by the assistance of Kamadeva, the god of love, who, at the instigation of the gods, shot Shiva with his arrow of love as he was engaged in meditation, while Parvati was in front of him, praying that her wish be gratified. Shiva opened his eyes and fell in love with Parvati.

According to a legend, when Shiva raised the dead body of Sati in his arms he began to dance in a frantic manner. The earth trembled beneath the weight of such a load; and Vishnu, fearing there would be an utter destruction of the universe if this were allowed to continue, let fly his *chakra* (discus), and cut Sati's body into fifty-one pieces. These fell in different places, a leg here, a hand there; but wherever a part touched the earth, the spot became sacred as a *shakti-peetha*. Temples or shrines have been made at these places. The renowned temple at Kali Ghat, near Kolkata, for example, is said to possess the big toe of her left foot.

Parvati is represented in pictures as a fair and beautiful woman, with no superfluity of limbs. Few miraculous deeds are claimed for her. It is when she appears as Durga, that she manifests divine powers, and exhibits a very different spirit from that which she has in her as Parvati.

Durga

The consort of Shiva now assumes a very different character from that in which she has so far been represented. In those incarnations, though as the wife of Shiva, she acted as an ordinary woman, and manifested womanly virtues; as Durga she was a most powerful warrior, and appeared on earth, under many names, for the destruction of demons who were obnoxious to gods and men.

She obtained the name Durga because she slew an *asura* named Durg, the name of the goddess being the feminine form of the demon's name. According to the Skanda Purana a giant named Durg, the son of Ruru, having performed penance in favour of Brahma, obtained his blessings, and grew so mighty that he conquered the three worlds, and dethroned Indra and the other gods. The gods in their distress appealed to Shiva, who asked Parvati to go and destroy this giant. She, accepting the commission willingly, calmed the fears of the gods, and first sent Kalaratri (Dark Night), a female whose beauty bewitched the inhabitants of the three worlds, to order the demon to restore things back to normal. He, however, full of fury, sent his soldiers to lay hold of Kalaratri; but by the breath of her mouth she reduced them to ashes. Durg then sent giants, who were such monsters in size that they covered the surface of the earth. At the sight of these giants, Kalaratri fled to Parvati, followed by the giants. There was a fierce battle between Durg the *asura* and Parvati. The *asura* used many celestial

weapons, took the form of an elephant and then a buffalo, but Parvati vanquished him and his army easily. In his final true form he was picked up by Parvati and thrown on the ground very forcefully, with his chest pierced by an arrow and mouth spewing blood. The gods were delighted at the result, and soon regained their former splendour.

Still another account of the origin of Durga is found in the Vamana Purana. When the gods sought Vishnu in their distress, he, Shiva, Brahma, and the other gods, emitted such flames from their eyes that a mountain of effulgence was formed, which became manifest as Katyayini, refulgent as a thousand suns, having three eyes, black hair, and eighteen arms. Shiva gave her a trident, Vishnu a discus, Varuna a conch-shell, Agni a dart, Vayu a bow, Surya a quiver full of arrows, Indra a thunderbolt, Kubera a mace, Brahma a rosary and water-pot, Kala a shield and sword, Vishwakarma a battleaxe and other weapons. Thus armed, and adored by the gods,

Katyayini proceeded to the Vindhya hills. Whilst there, the *asuras* Chanda and Manda saw her, and being captivated by her beauty they so described her to Mahishasur (also known as Durg), their king, that he was anxious to obtain her. On asking for her hand, she told him she must be won in a fight. They fought; at length the goddess dismounted from her lion, and sprang upon the back of Mahishasur, who was in the form of a buffalo, and with her feet so smote him on the head that he fell to the ground senseless, and then she cut off his head with her sword. Hence she is also known as Mahishasurmardini.

The Durga image is represented as a golden-coloured woman, with a gentle and beautiful countenance. She has ten arms; in one hand she holds a spear, with which she is piercing the giant Mahishasura; with one of her left hands she holds the tail of a serpent, with another the hair of the giant whose breast the snake is biting; her other hands are filled with various weapons. Her lion

leans against her right leg, and the giant against her left.

In Bengal the worship of this goddess, or Durga *puja*, is the most popular of all the Hindu festivals. Sacrifices of buffaloes and goats are made to her; feasting, singing and dancing are continued throughout the ten days, especially the last three days of the period of *navaratri*. Though her chief festival is in autumn, she is also worshipped in spring. The reason of this seems that Ravana was a devout worshipper of Durga, and had the Chandi (an extract from one of the Puranas) read daily. When, therefore, Rama attacked him, the goddess assisted her servant Ravana. It was in spring that Ravana observed her festival. Rama, seeing the help his enemy received from this goddess, began himself to worship her. This was in autumn. Durga was delighted with the devotion of Rama, and at once transferred her aid to him. The day of Durga's epic victory is celebrated as *vijayadashami*, coinciding with Rama's victory over Ravana.

The Chief Forms Of Durga

DURGA received Chanda and Manda, the messengers of the giants. They, struck with her beauty, spoke so rapturously of her to their lords that Sumbha sent her an offer of marriage by Sugriva.

DASABHUJA (the ten-handed) destroyed Sumbha's army under the commander-in-chief Dhumlochana. Of these troops only a few fugitives escaped to carry the news of their defeat to their master.

SINGHAVAHINI (riding on a lion) fought with Chanda and Manda, and has four arms only. She drank the blood of the leaders, and devoured a large part of their troops.

MAHISHASURMARDINI (the slayer of Mahishasur) slew Sumbha as he attacked her in the form of a buffalo. She had eight or, according to other accounts, ten arms. There is little to distinguish the account of this form from that of Durga.

JAGADDHATRI (the mother of the world) destroyed another army of the giants; is dressed in red garments, and is seated on a lion. She too, has four arms only, and is very similar to Singhavahini; the difference being in the weapons she wields. As Singhavahini, she carries a sword and spear, and with two hands is encouraging her worshippers; as Jagaddhatri, she carries a conch-shell, discus, bow and arrow. In all the above forms she is represented as a fair, beautiful, gentle-looking goddess.

KALI (the black goddess), or, as she is more commonly called Kali Ma, the black mother, with the aid of Chandi, slew Raktavija, the main leader of the giant's army. Seeing his men fall, Raktavija attacked the goddess in person; when from every drop of blood that fell from his body a thousand giants equal in power to himself arose. At this crisis another form of the goddess, named Chandi, came to the rescue. As Kali drank the giant's blood and prevented the formation of new giants, Chandi slew the monster herself.

Kali is represented as a black goddess with four arms; in one hand she has a sword, in another the head of the giant she has slain, with the other two she is encouraging her worshippers. For earrings she has two dead bodies; wears a necklace of skulls; her only clothing is a girdle made of dead men's hands, and her tongue protrudes from her mouth. Her eyes are red as those of a drunkard, and her face and breasts are besmeared with blood. She stands with one foot on the thigh, and another on the breast of her husband. This position of Kali is accounted for by the fact that, after her victory over the giants, she danced with joy so furiously that the earth trembled beneath her weight. At the request of the gods, Shiva asked her to desist, but owing to her excitement, she did not notice him. So he lay down amongst the slain. She continued dancing until she caught sight of her husband under her feet, and then immediately thrust out her tongue with shame at the disrespect she had shown him; and stopped.

MUKTAKESI (having flowing hair) destroyed another part of the giant's forces. In appearance there is little to distinguish her from Kali: she has four arms; holds a sword and a shield in her left hands, and with her right she is bestowing a blessing and dispelling fear. She too, is standing upon the body of her husband.

TARA (the saviour) slew Sumbha, and holds his head in one hand and a sword in another. Her appearance too, is similar to that of Kali. She must not be confused with Tara, the wife of Brihaspati; or Tara, the wife of Bali, the *asura* king.

CHINNAMASTAKA (the beheaded) slew Nisumbha, the other giant. It is evident from her appearance that she found her task rather difficult, for her head is half-severed from her body. She is painted as a fair woman, naked, and wearing a garland of skulls, standing upon the body of her husband Shiva.

JAGADGAURI (the yellow goddess) received the thanks and praises of the gods and men for the deliverance she brought. In her four hands she holds a conch-shell, a discus, a mace and a lotus.

PRATYANGIRA (the well-proportioned one). Of this form of Durga no images are made, but at night the officiating priest, wearing red clothes, offers red flowers, liquors, and bloody sacrifices. The flesh of animals dipped in some intoxicating drink is burned by the worshipper, believing that the flesh of the enemy for whose injury the ceremony is performed will swell, as the flesh of the sacrifice swells in the fire.

ANNAPURNA (one who gives food) is represented as a fair woman, standing on a lotus, or as sitting on a throne. In one hand she holds a rice bowl, and in the other a spoon used for stirring rice

GANESHAJANANI (mother of Ganesha) is worshipped with her infant in her arms.

KRISHNAKRORA (she who holds Krishna on her breast). When Krishna fought with the serpent Kaliya in the river Yamuna, he was bitten, and in pain called upon Durga for help. She heard his cry, and by suckling him from her breast, restored him to health.

Ganga

The River Ganga, is one of world's four and India's seven sacred rivers. The early Aryans worshipped Ganga as one of several river goddesses. Ganga gradually became the primary river goddess, subject of numerous legends, and endowed with fabulous qualities. The principle centres for the worship of Ganga are Gangotri, the source of the river; Haridwar, where she comes down to the plains; Allahabad, where she joins the Yamuna; Varanasi, the holy city; and Sagara Island in her estuary where she finally flows into the Bay of Bengal.

Ganga is supposed to be the daughter of Himavat and Mena, the older sister of Parvati. According to the Puranas, the heavenly Ganga flows from Vishnu's toe. Ganga sometimes assumes a human form. In one such appearance, she married King Shantanu and was the mother of Bhishma, *pitamah* to the warring Pandava and Kaurava clans.

Sagara was a mighty king of Ayodhya. He decided to perform the Ashvamedha in a bid to become king of the gods. He appointed his 60,000 sons to follow the horse. Meanwhile Indra, fearing the loss of his throne, disguised himself as a demon and scared away the horse. When Sagara's sons discovered this, they set out to locate the horse. During their search, they disrupted Sage Kapila's meditation. The sage cursed them and they were burnt to ashes. With no news from his sons, Sagara sent his grandson, Anshuman, to look for the horse. In the course of his search, he came upon the ashes of his father and uncles. When he discovered the reason for their destruction, Anshuman appeased Sage Kapila, who agreed to modify his curse. He told Anshuman that the souls of his uncles would be

sanctified if Ganga with her purifying touch flowed over their ashes. Meanwhile Anshuman found the horse and returned it to Sagara, who completed his sacrifice.

Sagara, Anshuman, and Anshuman's son Dilip all made unsuccessful attempts to liberate their kinsmen from Kapila's curse. Eventually the task came to Dilip's son, Bhagiratha.

By practicing severe austerities, Bhagiratha obtained a boon from Brahma to allow Ganga to come down to earth. However Bhagiratha was warned that Ganga would not want to leave heaven and therefore descend in a rage. The earth would not be able to sustain the impact of her fall and could disintegrate. Bhagiratha then prayed to Shiva, who agreed to sustain her descent on his head. Accordingly, Brahma told Ganga to go down to earth, which she resented. She swept down in fury, bent on destruction, but Shiva caught her in the coils of his hair and held her fast. When her anger subsided, he let her flow. In one of her seven streams, Ganga followed Bhagiratha and flowed over the ashes of Sagara's sons, releasing their souls.

According to the Agni Purana, any place where Ganga flows becomes sacred. It is believed that even hardened criminals and sinners will go to heaven if they worship the Ganga. The water of Ganga is graced with extraordinary properties of purification and does not putrify even after years of being kept in bottles and jars. Even today, Ganga continues to draw millions of devotees to her banks, and her water is carried back in small, sealed pots and reverentially placed in innumerable household shrines across India. Ganga being Divine Consciousness, whoever immerses himself in it becomes immortal. It is eternal because it is the highest consciousness, which human beings are capable of attaining during their spiritual endeavour. Ganga symbolically represents divine and esoteric knowledge with the powers to elevate the dead as well as the living towards heavens, with the strength of its purity.

Gayatri

According to the sacred texts, Gayatri is Brahma, Gayatri is Vishnu, Gayatri is Shiva, Gayatri is the Vedas. Gayatri is a metre of the Rig-Veda consisting of 24 syllables. This metre has been used in a number of Rig Vedic *mantras*. The syllables are arranged differently for different *mantras*, the most common being a triplet of eight syllables each. The Gayatri *mantra* composed in this triplet form is the most famous and sacred of all *mantras*. It is a prayer in honour of the Sun, also called Savitur. According to the Skanda Purana, nothing in the Vedas is superior to Gayatri.

She is another consort of Lord Brahma. According to one interpretation, the goddess Gayatri is the luminous emanation of the infinite power of the Original One in three aspects in the three parts of the day; as Gayatri in the morning, as Savitri at noon and as Saraswati in the evening. As the goddess of learning she is sometimes said to be the daughter of Brahma, the original creator emanating from his mind (*manasa-kanya*). In the worship of Durga in autumn, Lakshmi and Saraswati accompany her as her two daughters.

She is shown as having five heads and is usually seated on a lotus, swan or a peacock. She is wearing crowns on all five heads; the crowns bear nine types of gems, which signify Divine Light. The four heads of Gayatri represent the four Vedas, the fifth head represents the almighty God.

Saraswati

Saraswati, goddess of speech, literally means the essence of one's own self. Saraswati denotes that aspect of the Supreme Reality which represents knowledge, learning, and wisdom. She is considered as the personification of all the arts, sciences, crafts, music, and poetry. The mother of all Vedic knowledge, she is also known as Vac, the goddess of river-like flowing speech. Saraswati is the divine consort of Brahma, the Lord of creation. Since knowledge is necessary for creation, Saraswati symbolizes the creative power of Lord Brahma.

Saraswati is the first river who was granted status as a Vedic goddess. Originally, from Central Asia, the Aryans were fire worshippers. Their tribes came into India around 1,500 BC and they settled along the banks of the Saraswati. The Saraswati, flowed from the Himalayas into the Indian Ocean, and she weaned the Aryans from their nomadic living to farming. Her fertile presence conferred them with rich harvests and prosperity. The sages and poets meditated along the banks of the Saraswati, and their muse became a goddess.

She is seen as a beautiful and elegant presence, pure white in colour, clad in a white sari, seated on a white lotus, representing purity and brilliance. She is depicted with four hands. In one hand she holds a book and in the other a rosary. With her other two hands, she is seen playing the *veena*. Her *vahana* is the swan and sometimes a peacock is

shown accompanying her. The swan is known for its exceptional characteristic of being capable of separating out water from milk, indicating that one should possess discrimination to segregate the bad from the good. Like the swan, the lotus seat of the goddess suggests her transcendence of the physical world. She floats above the muddy imperfections of the physical world, unsullied, pure and beautiful. Although rooted in the mud (like man is rooted in the physical world), the lotus perfects itself in a blossom that has transcended the mud. She inspires people to live in such a way that they may transcend their physical limitations through the ongoing creation.

Like Brahma, she is not worshipped much in temples. However, Goddess Saraswati is worshiped throughout India on her special day in spring, the Vasant Panchmi.

Lakshmi

The goddess Sri, who is also commonly known as Lakshmi is the consort of Lord Vishnu. She is associated with prosperity, well-being, royal power, and illustriousness. Lakshmi in the Hindu pantheon of gods and goddesses is personified as the goddess of fortune and also as the embodiment of grace and charm.

Ashta Lakshmi are her eight forms which are the commonly worshipped aspects. In each form, she bestows one form of wealth to her devotees. There are not as many temples for Lakshmi as are

for Parvati; she is however worshipped in temples, more so in the north of India. There are numerous *poojas* and festivals which are performed to invoke her blessings. The Ashta Lakshmis are: Aadi Lakshmi, Santana Lakshmi, Gaja Lakshmi, Dhana Lakshmi, Dhaanya Lakshmi, Vijaya Lakshmi, Veera Lakshmi and Aishwarya Lakshmi.

Lakshmi lived in the ocean and was discovered by Vishnu her husband in his *avatara* as a tortoise. When the *devas* (minor gods) were in race against the *asuras* (demons) to obtain *amrit* (the nectar of immortality); they decided to churn the ocean.

They created a churn by threading the serpent Vasuki around Mount Mandara. Vishnu, in the *avatara* of Kurma, dived to the ocean floor and balanced Mount Mandara on his back. In the grip of Kurma's cosmic clutch, the mountain could not sink into the ocean bed. The gods churned and received the nectar of immortality and other treasures. For Kurma the most precious was Lakshmi, the goddess of beauty and good fortune.

Vishnu carried Lakshmi from the ocean and married her first in heaven and then many times on earth. Each time Vishnu descended on earth in an *avatara*, he would marry an *avatara* of Lakshmi. A cosmic couple, they would wed on earth as in heaven. When Vishnu appeared as Parashurama, he married Lakshmi as Dharini. When he was Rama, Lakshmi was born as Sita. As Krishna he married her as Rukmini.

Lakshmi plays a central role in creation, for she

is Vishnu's *shakti*. Her birth from the ocean bestowed her with boundless fertility. On earth she is also known as *prakriti*, nature, the mother of all living beings.

Lakshmi is depicted in a female form with four arms. She wears a red saree with a golden border and is standing on a lotus. She has golden coins and lotuses in her hands. Two elephants are shown next to the goddess. The four arms represent the four directions in space and thus symbolize omnipresence and omnipotence of the goddess. The red colour symbolizes activity. The golden border on her saree denotes prosperity. The idea conveyed here is that the goddess is always busy distributing wealth and prosperity to the devotees. The lotus seat, which Lakshmi is standing upon, signifies that while living in this world, one should enjoy its wealth, but not become obsessed with it. Such a living is analogous to a lotus that grows in water but is not wetted by water. The two elephants standing next to the goddess symbolize the name and fame associated with worldly wealth. The idea conveyed here is that a true devotee should not earn wealth merely to acquire name and fame or only to satisfy his own material desires, but should share it with others in order to bring happiness to them as well.

Goddess Lakshmi is regularly worshipped in home shrines and temples by her devotees. A special worship is offered to her annually on the auspicious day of Diwali, with religious rituals and colorful ceremonies specifically devoted to her.

Radha

Radha is mostly represented as willingly subordinating herself to her lover Krishna, her personality dissolving into his. With her eyes closed the goddess follows him wherever he takes her, trusting him completely and giving up her ego. This is the divine metaphor of a devotee merging with her deity. By extension this is also symbolic of a lover merging in his beloved. In some representations the relationship of Radha and Krishna is reciprocal. Their depictions express fully matured love in which trust and respect for each other are so deep that disrespect is unimaginable. Such images suggest that when two people are in love, a merging of minds and bodies takes place, egos are abandoned and lover and beloved are equal in status. It not only sublimates the sexual emotions but also gives divine support to the inner passions. Radha's divine nature lies in exaltation and transfiguration of some of the most basic and archetypal of human emotions. Two of her characteristics: *mahabhava* (great feeling) and *premabhakti* (devotion of self-less love) point to the intensity and purity of her love giving it a metaphysical quality. Radha's devotees do not typically relate to her by petitioning her for earthly favours; but by becoming absorbed in the unfolding of minutely detailed story of her love for Krishna.

Sita

Sita means 'furrow' or the line made by a plough, and is the name of the goddess associated with ploughed fields in Vedic literature. In Ramayana, Sita as Rama's consort, is first and foremost a model of a dedicated wife and mistress of vegetation and forested places.

Sita's birth is supernatural and her abilities and appearance are exalted throughout the epic. Her father Janak found her while ploughing a field. She echoes many of her mother Prithvi's attributes: life-giving, fertile and fragrant earth mother, yet the dangers inherent in the one who creates and nourishes are also suggested. Sita, the fertility goddess, emerges from the earth and after all the trials and tribulations in her earthly life; goes back into it, thus signifying the necessity of death for life in the ecosystem.

Sita, the ideal wife, epitomizes the concept of *pativrata*, which literally means a virtuous woman who is faithful to her husband. The hardships and manifold accomplishments of a *pativrata* are highly esteemed. Although other goddesses such as Parvati and Lakshmi express many of these qualities, Sita by far is the most popular and beloved paradigm of wifely devotion, forbearance and chastity. Though considered as a deity, Sita is rarely worshipped in her own right. There are no temples dedicated to her alone; she is always seen in the company of her husband Rama and his brother Lakshmana.

Minor Gods

The Hindu Trinity and its extended family have the legendary heroes of the Puranas also added to it and elevated to the status of lesser or minor gods.

Bali is the grandson of Prahalad, and a devotee of Vishnu. Though a king of demons, he ruled with righteousness and the welfare of the subjects at heart. Having agreed to give in charity three paces of land to Vishnu, who came in the form of Vamana, Bali kept his promise by offering his head on which Vishnu could put his third step.

Dhruva is the grandson of Manu. He was five years old when he was insulted by his stepmother. He went to the forest in search of God and with determination and devotion he succeeded. Vishnu raised him to the skies as the Pole Star.

Eklavya worshipped a clay idol of his Guru, and practiced archery in his absence mastering the art. When his master desired the thumb of Ekalavya's right hand as a fee, which would have crippled him, Ekalavya smilingly complied.

Harishchandra, with his vow to remain truthful at all times, successfully faced the rigorous challenge posed by Vishwamitra. Though a king, he sacrificed everything he had at the altar of truth, including his kingdom, and even his son.

Kamadeva, the god of love, is very fair and handsome. Generally described as the son of Lakshmi and Vishnu, he is also said to be the son of Brahma. Kamadeva carries a bow made of sugarcane and strung with a line of humming bees. He shoots with his bow the five flower-tipped arrows of desire. Rati (passion) is his wife, Vasanta (spring) his friend and a parrot his vehicle. Shiva burned him to ashes as a punishment for disturbing his deep meditation, but Kamadeva's arrow had done the deed; Shiva fell in love with Parvati. Then responding to the pleas of his widow, Rati, Shiva restored her husband but only as a mental image, representing true love and affection and not just physical lust. Hence the other name of Kamadeva is Ananga (the body-less). After a very long period, Shiva finally allowed him to be born as the son of Krishna.

Kubera is the god of wealth. He is dwarfish, has three legs and eight teeth, has two to four hands and may carry in his hands a mace, a purse containing money, a vase, a fruit and a bowl and two hands in the boon giving and protective modes. His fair body is covered with jewels and other ornaments. His vehicle is a chariot called Pushpak. He is also called the gods of *yakshas*. His brother Ravana, by practicing austerities, obtained from Shiva the boon of invincibility and so was able to defeat Kubera and to seize Lanka and the chariot, Pushpak. As Lanka could not be restored to Kubera, Vishwakarma, the god of architecture, built him a palace on Mount Kailash in the Himalayas. Kubera is the guardian of the North, watching over the earth's mineral wealth of gold, silver, jewels, pearls etc.

Manu means 'the man' and he was created by Brahma. This name also belongs to fourteen mythological progenitors of mankind. It is believed that it was the seventh Manu who saved the world from deluge with the help of the Matsya *avatara* of Vishnu.

Nachiketa sought knowledge at a very tender age. By his humility he won over the heart of Yama the god of death and learnt the secrets of spiritual life from him.

Prahlad was the son of the demon-king Hiranyakashipu. He faced the anger of his mighty father for the sake of his faith in Lord Vishnu. Poison, sword and fire could not frighten him. And then the Lord himself responded to the devotion of the five-year old boy and came to the earth as Narasimha.

Savitri was the daughter of king Ashwapati, not to be confused with the consort of Brahma. She insisted on having a noble young man Satyavan for her husband, though she knew he had only a year to live. On the fatal day, she followed Yama, the god of death, as he carried away her husband's life. Finally Yama bowed to her love and devotion, and restored her husband back to life.

Soma is the moon god also known as Chandra. He is said to be the son of Dharma or of Varuna, lord of oceans, from which the moon rises. Soma is identified with *amrit* (nectar). He is represented as a copper coloured man, trailing a red pennant behind his three wheeled chariot, which is drawn either by an antelope or by ten white horses. He has normally four hands, one

carrying a mace, second carrying *amrit*, the third carrying a lotus and the last in a protective mode. It is believed that during half the month, thirty six thousand divinities feed on Soma and thus assure their immortality; accounting for the waxing and waning of the moon.

Vishwakarma, according to Rig Veda, is the divine architect of the whole universe. He is the personification of the creative power that joins heaven and earth. He is the son of Brahma and is the architect of all the gods' palaces. He is fair, has a club in his right hand, wears a crown, a necklace of gold, rings on his fingers and holds tools in his left hand. All the flying chariots of the gods; all their weapons are his creation. It was Vishwakarma who built the golden city of Lanka, over which King Ravana ruled and built the city of Dwarka, the capital of Lord Krishna. Again it was he who revealed the Sthapathya Veda, or the science of mechanics and architecture. It was his blessings that enabled Nala, the monkey, to build the bridge of stones over the sea for Lord Rama and his army to reach Lanka. According to a legend his daughter Sanjana was married to Surya, the sun. As she was not able to endure the heat and light of the sun, Vishwakarma cut away an eighth part of his brightness. The fragments were used by him to form the weapons for the major gods: discus for Vishnu, trident for Shiva, sword for Kartikeya etc. He is the presiding deity of all craftsmen.

Yama is the god of death and is the lord of the infernal regions visited by man after cessation of life. He is the embodiment of the law of *karma* and imparts justice according to deeds. Yama is the son of Vivasvat, the embodiment of social morality, while his mother is Saranyu (cloud), daughter of Vishwakarma, the cosmic architect. Yama's twin sister is Yami, who later appeared on this earth as the river Yamuna. Yama is the guardian of the South and is called Dakshinaspati. His abode is named as Yamalaya on the southern side of the earth. To the virtuous and to the sinner Yama appears in different forms. To the virtuous he appears to be like Vishnu. He has four arms, a dark complexion and lotus shaped eyes. His face is charming and he wears a resplendent smile. In the case of the wicked, he is seen with long limbs, deep eyes, large teeth and thin black lips. He roars like the ocean of destruction. Yama's mount is a fierce-looking black buffalo. Yama has several wives, the three main ones being, Hemamala (golden garland), Sushila (good-natured one), and Vijaya (victory).

Celestial beings often mentioned in the various Vedas and Puranas are as much a part of the Hindu mythology as the minor gods.

Apsaras are beautiful women, who dance in the court of Indra. Indra also uses them to lure the sages who by their severe penance endanger his superiority as the ruler of Swarga (paradise). Rambha, Urvashi and Menaka are the most celebrated of them.

Gandharvas are the celestial musicians who play in the court of Indra and also when some divine act of the gods has been completed in the interest of humanity. They are said to be exceptionally handsome and have a great fondness for women.

Kinnaras are mythical beings, with a body of a man and head of a horse. They are singers at the court of Indra. They are also sometimes said to be the minstrels of Kubera's palace at Mount Kailash, which is also the abode of Shiva.

Siddhas are classes of spirits of great purity and holiness, who dwell alone in the sky or mid-air between earth and heaven.

Yakshas are the attendants of Kubera, employed to guard his gardens and treasure. They live in Alka-Puri (*yaksha-puri*). The female of *yaksha* is known as *yakshini*.